Even Though

Kory W. Nelson

CONTENTS

Even Though

Incarceration without rehabilitation is not only wrong, it is sickening, and yes it is sick, indeed, because incarceration is not rehabilitation. In fact, I guess you could say that it is a definition of a defamation of one's character; treating an addict who is addicted to narcotics like your everyday common criminal, and locking them up in the same cage as real, actual, violent criminals. Our legal justice system is flawed, because having a substance abuse problem and being an addict does not make you a criminal, but yet we treat them like they are. Putting accused murderers and other violent offenders in the same pod as non-violent drug addicts is not okay, and this happened almost every time that I went to jail, during classification, which is what happens after being booked. You go through the process of being classified to see if you have any gang affiliation, or if you are prone to violence based off your current or past charges, and any infractions you may have had in the past while in jail. Sometimes it can take several days, if not weeks, before you get moved from classification. Each time I went to jail during Covid, there was a ten-day quarantine requirement, so you were stuck in classification for at least ten days. If you physically hurt other people, then I agree, those people should be locked up behind bars, but please tell me, how is it just-us (justice), "Even Though" the only ones we are physically harming is just us.

The world has criminalized addiction. It is not enough just to call them drug addicts; if you get caught with the drugs you are addicted to in your possession, then in the eyes of the law you are a criminal. If you are addicted to hard drugs then that's one thing, but for people that are hooked on pharmaceuticals, oftentimes the only difference between catching a felony possession of a controlled substance charge and being let go is a piece of paper that has a prescription written on it. Many people start out doing those pills with their own names written on that paper, and they may get cut off from that medication for whatever reason. Just because someone gets cut off doesn't mean they aren't still addicted to it, and there is no guarantee that they aren't going to go and try to find some on the street. Many people turn to the hard drugs when they can no longer find the medication that they used to get prescribed. If they do go and find someone with pills on the street, I wonder if a thought goes through their head that, wow, I just went from being a law-abiding citizen to possibly catching a felony drug charge, just that fast, in a matter of seconds. The problem with buying pills from the street, though, is many people think the pills they are buying are legit, because they look just like the medication they normally take. But almost all the pills on the streets nowadays are fake, counterfeit, lookalike pills that are often cut with drugs like Fentanyl. You might not even know it is has Fentanyl in it, so you take it just like your normal medication, and it could kill you. You could overdose and die from taking just one pill. This is not even a hypothetical scenario; this happens every day, in real life, in America. I know people who have lost their lives, and have friends who have lost a family member, that way.

A lot of people will say that jail is not too bad, and it is necessary for people who break the law to go there; and yeah jail does serve a purpose, but that doesn't mean it's not a scary and dangerous place, because it is. And you best believe that for a first time offender who has never been in trouble before in their entire life, when they walk into jail for the first time, it is absolutely intimidating. Everyone is always angry and on edge because they are being held against their will, and they don't want to be there. So if you disrespect them or if you make their lives more uncomfortable at all, or even if you are just looking at someone the perceived "wrong way," then you are going to get hurt. There are two sets of rules inside a jail, there are the facility rules, and then there are the inmate rules.

If you break the facility rules, you will be punished and most likely sent to the "hole," which is also known as segregation, where you get put in a cell by yourself and are basically on twenty-three-and-a-half-hours of lockdown every day, and lose all of your privileges. Time goes by even slower in there.

If you break the unwritten inmate rules, there will be physical consequences. It is not a game, and they are not playing around. I have seen people in there get hurt, badly, like had to be taken to a hospital by an ambulance badly. The first couple of times I went to jail for having drugs and being an addict, I was honestly terrified, like I wouldn't even leave my cell.

Then I would get released with no treatment plan, and as soon as I got out, I would go pick up and get right back to using my drugs. In fact, I never had a discussion with any jail employees ever about resources that were available, or how I could get into a treatment program. The more times I got arrested, the more comfortable I got going to jail and being in that environment. After being in there a few times, I started to come out of my cell and started talking to people, making connections and getting their numbers, so that I could reach out and expand my horizon in the drug world. My contact list grew each time I went to jail, and every time I got out, I could now find my drugs even cheaper than I could when I got arrested. If we are going to incarcerate people and take their freedom away from them for simply being an addict and having the drugs on them that they are addicted to, then can we please at least have a conversation about how to fix the problem, and come up with an actual solution, because the system in place right now is not the answer. This is not a one size fits all solution to the problem.

In theory, yeah, it sounds like a good idea to arrest people who are addicted to drugs and put them in jail so they get clean, and are away from the drugs, so they start to detox, and then go into recovery. The problem is, though, in reality, almost every jail in America has drugs in it. So, are we really helping them if we lock people up to get them away from their addiction if they can still find it and get high behind bars? If an addict knows they can get access to the drug they are addicted to or something like it, they will do anything to make it happen, and I do mean anything. If there is a will, there is a way, and if they do happen to get high behind bars, the likelihood of them overdosing is much higher because they are trying to hide the fact they have something they aren't supposed to have, and their tolerance is way down from what it normally is.

I was given a Fentanyl pill while in jail, ended up overdosing, and woke up in the hospital. So I know from personal experience just how prevalent the drugs are inside the jails, and just how dangerous, and possibly deadly, it could be. I had to be taken to the hospital from jail on four separate occasions, because my vitals were so low from detoxing, and I was bleeding internally from all of the drug abuse and it almost killed me. The body scanners nowadays do help a lot, but to think that is going to stop one hundred percent of the drugs coming into the facility is just naïve thinking.

Putting a non-violent first time offender in jail, who is an addict and got caught with drugs, and is about to go through a withdrawal, is like throwing a scared, little, sick puppy into a cage with full grown, mean, big dogs. We all have heard the saying that when someone is going to attack you your mind goes into fight or flight mode. Well in jail, it's either fight or die, because you can't "flight" since you're locked in a cage and there is nowhere to run.

We need to find better ways to deal with these sick people that are battling their disease of addiction, day in and day out. And I promise you, they are sick. If you were to go and ask most opioid users if they want to go and get high, they will tell you no, they want to go get well. The reason for this is, after using the drug for a little while, your body quickly begins building up a tolerance to it. And once that happens your body needs more of it, and both your mind and body become addicted to it. Your entire mindset changes from a want mentality to an absolute must-have mentality, just to feel normal.

Addicts feel like they desperately need to get their fix, and "Even Though" they are breaking the law, they are doing so just to try to get their "medicine" to feed their addiction. Now I'm not excusing anyone breaking the law, I'm simply explaining to you why they are breaking the law. Anyone who has never dealt with addiction, trust me, you will never get it, but if you think that putting drug addicts in jail over simple possession or drug paraphernalia is the answer to that problem, then you are sadly mistaken. Take it from me. I have been to multiple jails, in two different states, due to my addiction. While some jails were nicer than others, there was always one thing they all had in common: all jails have the same tough, hate culture. Jails are literally a hate factory that teach you to suppress all of your emotions and either shut down and become silent, or, if you do decide to speak out, then it will be all hate or anger coming out of your mouth. This is because you are taught right when you get to jail that there ain't no crying in jail, and that it is not okay to show real emotion in there besides anger, and if you do cry or show emotion, then you are considered a punk, or even worse, a bitch. Once you get that rep in jail, you're going to wish you had just kept quiet, because now, let's just say, you're going to have a rough time for the remainder of your stay.

So again, I ask the question: Why do people who are suffering from addiction get treated like your everyday common criminal, because news flash: jail is absolutely, unequivocally, a gateway into the criminal underworld. What do you think is going to happen when you take someone who is withdrawing and coming down from drugs, and is a drug addict, and you lock them in the same room as other drug users, drug dealers, and also other users who are actually criminals? You are giving that vulnerable drug addict new ways and new methods to break the law, and new schemes to make money, to buy and trade for drugs to support their addiction. You think you're actually helping society by doing this? Hell no, you're not. In fact, you're literally just throwing more fuel onto the fire.

Addiction is not a choice, it's a disease. Choosing to get high is a choice, choosing to hang out with criminals and learn their behavior in order to get your drugs easier is also a choice. But you know what else is a choice as well? Choosing to send that person to some kind of treatment facility instead of jail, where they meet those criminals in the first place. We have to develop a new system where, when people who are suffering from addiction get arrested for simple possession or drug paraphernalia, instead of sending them to jail, either put them into some kind of treatment facility, or, if they do have to go to jail, then put them on some kind of treatment plan coming out of jail. The system in place right now is ridiculous, because they are literally just arresting people, putting them in jail, and then just releasing them. It's like fishing, just catch and release on a never ending cycle. They release them and then hope they will be what, like miraculously reincarnated? Probably not. Honestly, chances are more like reincarcerated. The recidivism rate is out of control. Obviously, this is not working. It's the same twenty percent of people, eighty percent of the time.

The definition of insanity is doing the same thing over and over again and expecting a different result. So are our lawmakers insane then? No, I just believe that they are misinformed, and could humbly learn a thing or two from people who have lived with addiction and overcame the odds that were stacked against them, which is not an easy thing to do, especially when our system is as flawed as it is in regard to how we treat people who are struggling with addiction or other mental health issues.

The jails nowadays are basically having to act as both a detention center as well as a mental health facility, and they are not equipped to do so. Half of the people in jail should not even be in jail, because they are not criminals, they are just dealing with some mental health issues and should be in a mental health facility somewhere instead.

Imagine a world where when you get arrested for drugs and

paraphernalia, instead of being taken to a jail, you are taken to a detox facility, where you go through the withdrawal process under the direct supervision of medical professionals, in a facility that is actually designed for that purpose. You then get put on medically-assisted treatment, and then transition into a treatment program. You go from short term recovery, and work your program, and end up in long term recovery, which is actually when you start to get your life back.

There is a light and a certain type of glow that illuminates from people who have overcome their addiction. And seeing someone's flame starting to burn so bright again, after being in the dark for so long, truly is a special sight to see! We should not be putting that burden and added stress on the detention officers. Their job is already hard enough. Like straight up, those officers inside the detention facilities have to keep their head on a swivel at all times, because it is dangerous in there, and you never know when someone is going to snap and try to attack you. The detention officers have to pay special attention to the people detoxing, to make sure they are okay, but that distracts them from everything else going on around them in the pod.

You have a bunch of people who're coming down off of drugs, and you have a lot of people dealing with psychosis and are extremely paranoid, people who are not in their right mind and are not on the right medication, and when you try and mix them with the rest of the general population, around a bunch of real criminals who are all pissed off because they already don't want to be there, then you're just asking for all hell to break loose. And this is what jail is like every single day!

In our criminal justice system, if you have a substance abuse problem, then that front door turns into a revolving door, and the first and last people that the inmates see both entering and exiting the jail are the detention or correctional officers. To the officers: You can have a profound impact on the inmates who are coming through your facilities. Just some friendly advice: Try to keep it professional and don't mock people and tell them that you will see them again real soon when they are getting released, because they are just going to relapse, and end up right back in there. Try giving them some proactive words of encouragement to go and get into some kind of treatment program, so they can try to better themselves and hopefully not end up back in there. "Even Though" you may have just been joking with them, they don't take it that way. They look at your comments like they are rude and disrespectful, and it just makes them have even more resentment toward you, and the system as a whole. Although you might think we don't even hear you, I promise you, we hear every word. Even if you look at some of those people and think, wow, that person is just another lost cause, and you may be right, they may be lost, but they are still just that, a person. And in an environment where you feel almost dehumanized like jail, just try to have a little bit of empathy, and treat them with some humanity, because God knows these people are going through some true humility.

Think about how you would want one of your family members treated if they were going through that same difficult situation. A lot of people in jail don't have anyone on the outside who actually cares about them, so when someone shows that they actually give a damn, that can go a long way, because they don't care how much you know, until they know how much you care. Most of the officers do keep it professional, but there are always a couple of bad apples out there that always ruin it for everyone else.

The recidivism rate is so high, people literally get stuck in the system for years, sometimes their entire life, in and out of jail. We are products of our environment, and in that environment they will always try to drag you back down, because misery loves company. And once you are in the system, nobody cares about you, and you literally lose your identity as a person and become just another number to them.

Jail is all about respect. If you disrespect somebody, then you're going to get dealt with, and if you steal from anybody, or snitch on anyone, then you are probably going to end up in protective custody, because you are now a target for the entire pod, and you either roll out, or they will roll you out. There is a saying in jail that "the only thing worse than a jail-house thief is a jail-house rat."

For those addicts who have never been to jail before, they are in for a very rude awakening. Jail is not like anything you have experienced before, and it will change you. Most of the people who go to jail for the first time who are non-violent drug addicts are not criminals at first, but putting them in jail could turn them into a criminal. Jail doesn't rehabilitate you; it makes you angry, and, honestly, it makes you worse. After a while, you become institutionalized, and start to become desensitized to things that you should never become desensitized to, like having to get butt naked in front of strangers and having to bend over and squat and cough, sometimes in a room with up to ten other naked guys lined up in a row right next to you on the wall. I used to get so nervous and would get anxiety doing it, but after going to jail so many times because of my addiction, it got to the point where it didn't even faze me anymore, and became just a normal part of life. Which is actually really sad, because being seen naked by strangers, when you don't want to be seen naked by those strangers, is really embarrassing, and humiliating, and is beyond an invasion of privacy. I understand for security reasons why the officers need to strip search you, like they don't really have a choice, but why make you do it in front of all those other people? That is their choice. That only happened a few times, but it's a few times that I will never forget. All the other times, the strip searches were done in a private room, which is how it should be! At least that saves you a little bit of dignity.

I ask every parent or legal guardian out there to ask yourself this question: If your kid is struggling with a substance abuse problem and is addicted to drugs, is this really the type of place you would want them to have to go to in order to get help for their addiction, around a bunch of real criminals that will try to corrupt any part of them that they can, and are in a facility that doesn't actually rehabilitate them, and doesn't even get them on a treatment plan coming out?

Like what are we even doing? Our legal justice and mental health system in place right now truly is crazy, and needs a major overhaul. Let's reserve jail cells for those that actually deserve jail cells. We need to make treatment programs more accessible for people, which includes the affordability issue. I have been quoted thirty to fifty to one hundred thousand dollars for a bed in an inpatient rehab. They won't even let you set up a payment plan. You either pay it all up front, or you don't get in at all. We should not have to spend our life savings or go into debt just to try to save our loved one's life and get them into a treatment program. Every day matters, every hour, every minute could be the difference between life or death. It takes 30 seconds to get high. Time is of the essence, and the faster we take action on this, the more lives we are going to be able to save.

How did we even get into this criminalized opioid epidemic in the first place? I will tell you. All of this goes hand in hand. Why do you think the big pharma companies have to pay billions of dollars in damage settlements to the cities and states all over our country? It's because they are responsible for this deadly epidemic. They used corruption and coercion to flood our communities with their addictive poison. They pushed it onto our doctors, and pushed it into our hospitals, under the false misrepresentation, and flat out disgusting lie, that it was a miracle drug, and that it was low risk for abuse, and not addictive. They even got the FDA to sign off on it, which is when it really took off.

There for a while, it was like a feeding frenzy. People were doctor shopping, and going to pill mills and pain management clinics, and were getting multiple prescriptions from multiple doctors, and were having them filled at multiple pharmacies. Big Pharma created a demand for the pills, and made hundreds of billions of dollars from it. The DEA then came in and started regulating, and shut almost all of that down. Many people got cut off for trying to abuse the system, or their medication, and when they got cut off, many of them did end up turning to the streets trying to find some more. That's when it really got bad. I remember, for a while, it was a dollar per milligram on the streets for Oxy's.

The majority of crimes committed in this country are driven by our nation's drug problem. You fix the drug problem, you fix the crime problem. And when I say fix the drug problem, I'm not just talking about trying to stop all of the drugs coming in through our borders. That is extremely important as well and is a great start. And there are definitely a lot less drugs coming through our borders right now, which is a very good thing. But it's all about supply and demand. If you can get people who are hooked on drugs into treatment, then you can lower the demand, which will decrease the supply. As soon as it stops being lucrative for the drug dealers, they are going to stop selling it. It's all about the money to them. But we have to get the people who are already addicted to drugs into treatment programs. There are all kinds of different options for treatment: detox centers, rehabs, in-patient, out-patient, transition centers, sober living houses, sober outdoor retreats, medication-assisted treatment (MAT) programs, recovery residencies, halfway houses, and local programs and initiatives.

This opioid epidemic has impacted every city, state, and town in America, and big pharma is to blame, although I will give them credit for paying billions of dollars in damage settlements for the irreparable harm they have caused. Because of that huge influx of cash that our cities and states are receiving, we have a very unique opportunity to make some absolutely necessary changes to our criminal justice system and build a new network of mental health- and addiction-based treatment centers, and create an improved system that is designed to actually address the root causes of the crisis.

The number one problem for making these changes is always a lack of money and funding, but that is my point. They are getting money that does not come out of their budget, and has to be spent on opioid related programs and ideas. This is truly a once-in-a-lifetime opportunity, and if we act now on fixing the system, then we can help people for generations to come. They do not have to stay stuck in the same broken system like we had to. Let's get to the root causes and fix it, instead of just putting a band aid on it now and having to worry about it later. The longer we continue to put a band aid on an open wound, the more infected that wound will become.

For me, addiction started when I was 15 years old. I broke my wrist, and I started popping pills like they were candy. I became addicted to painkillers, and I didn't even know what addiction was. The day my prescription ran out is the day my life changed forever. All I could think about was how to get some more. I even contemplated hurting myself to try to get more. I went from popping pills to crushing them up and snorting them within a matter of weeks, because I was told they would hit me harder that way. I went through my pills so fast, I started stealing my dad's pain pills, and then when he caught me and confronted me about that, I went and started talking to people I would never have associated with if it weren't for me trying to find some more pills. When that failed, and I really got desperate, I went and started asking random strangers for pills on the street, which, many years later, led to a full-blown Fentanyl addiction. I come from a good family, with good morals. This can happen to anyone. That's what is so scary about it all. Don't think that this can't happen to you or your family or someone you care about, because it can, and it does, happen, every day, unfortunately.

What has been going on with the opioid epidemic since the early 2000s reminds me of another time in American History: Prohibition. On January 17th, 1920, the United States government made the manufacture, sale, and transportation of alcohol illegal, but federal law did not explicitly ban its consumption.

"Even Though" it was illegal now to the entire country, doctors could still legally prescribe whiskey or other liquors for various ailments, and pharmacies were still allowed to sell it. If you got caught with alcohol during Prohibition without a prescription, you would go to jail. This loophole became a booming business. Sound familiar? If history has taught us anything, it's that if people really want or need something, they are going to find a way to get it. It doesn't matter what the barriers are, they are going to find a loophole or do whatever they have to do to get around any laws or rules that there may be.

In the last fifteen years, nearly one million Americans have lost their lives to drug overdoses. One million people. That number absolutely breaks my heart. I started an LLC called Save One Life At A Time. I named it that because even one life lost is one too many. I want to try to help as many people as I possibly can, but my focus is to help save one life at a time, one person at a time. About three out of every four of those deaths involved opioids, with Fentanyl becoming the leading cause in recent years. Behind every statistic is a name, a face, and a story; someone's child, parent, friend, or partner. This epidemic has touched every community, and every kind of family, reminding us that addiction doesn't discriminate. But it also reminds us of something else: That recovery is possible, and every life saved is proof of that hope.

It took 13 years for Prohibition to end. When will this opioid epidemic end? Until we end the stigma around addiction and start treating people like they are sick with a disease instead of a criminal with a drug problem, things will never change.

While doing some research, I came across a term called "obsession of the mind." It's basically, changing out one thing your mind is addicted to for another. The stigma around addiction is awful, and people honestly oftentimes look down on addicts, whether they are currently struggling with addiction, or if they have in the past. I know this because I have been judged by people many times while sharing my story about my struggle.

Can addiction be a bad thing? Of course! More often than not, addiction is a terrible thing. But you can become addicted to anything. Some people are addicted to working out, others are addicted to eating healthy, some people are addicted to work, while others are addicted to making money; some people are addicted to becoming a better parent, while others are addicted to being a better teacher, doctor, lawyer, farmer, counselor, firefighter. While working on those things, sometimes people start to become addicted to food, coffee, their phones, TV, video games, sex, gambling, alcohol, tobacco, tattoos, sports. Some people are addicted to working on themselves, and becoming a better person; that is the current addiction I have. I used to be addicted to drugs, but I switched the obsession of my mind to something healthier. So next time you think about judging someone for their addiction, just ask yourself: Is there anything I'm addicted to? Even if you have an addiction to something healthy, moderation is important. If you don't want to call it an addiction, but you don't want to live without it, then call it an obsession of your mind instead.

There has to be a better way that we can deal with this issue, like c'mon y'all, we can do better than this! Why am I so sure of this? I'm sure, because damnit, this is *thee* United States of America! Land of the free and home of the brave. And not just our brave armed forces, who are the best and bravest in the world, but our brave teachers who do so much yet are paid so little, or the brave nurses who showed up to work day in, and day out, during the COVID-19 pandemic to take care of sick and scared patients, "Even Though" they were scared to death themselves.

Then there are the brave single mothers and fathers who are working full time while also struggling to keep the lights on and a roof over their family's head, and trying to raise their children to become good people; or the brave parents who are struggling financially, and trying to figure out which meals they can skip for themselves to make sure that their children miss none.

Bravery is standing up for and protecting the kid who is getting bullied and picked on at school. The veteran who is struggling with PTSD and depression, choosing to talk about it and look for support instead of taking drastic action. If that's not bravery, then I don't know what is. To the people who are doing the best they can, but acknowledge they are struggling and ask for help, you are brave.

At the end of the day, though, to me, bravery is about conquering our fears and finding a way to overcome what scares us the most. We all have the ability to be brave, but we have to decide for ourselves if we want to continue to grow and evolve into the person that we know we could be, or are we going to stay stuck, and let fear rule our lives? But I must warn you, if we are not growing, then we are rotting, and that will be our demise.

Bravery is also standing up for something you feel is wrong or unjust, because this is the best country in the world, and I'm damn proud to be an American. But nobody is perfect, and there is always room for improvement. Now, I'm only one voice, but if we unite and bring our voices together on this, it would be like the awakening of a sleeping giant, and "Even Though" they may call us defiant, good luck telling a defiant giant to be silent.

Society tells us, and teaches us, that if you see something, say something. Well guess what? I saw something, and now I'm saying something. I plan to go back to school, get my CDAC certification, and become a substance abuse counselor. I also want to go to high schools and talk to teens about drugs and the devastating impact they have had on my life. That is around the same age I was when all of my addiction problems started happening, which I feel is true for a lot of people who are just experimenting with things for the first time. If nobody really talks to them about it at that age, then how are they supposed to know how to handle it?

I think D.A.R.E. is a great program for kids, I really do, but that is done around 4th grade. I feel like there should be some kind of refresher course for high schools. So now I'm trying to do something about it, because now that I'm no longer blindfolded and contributing to the problem, I want to become part of the solution. Misery loves company, but success breeds success, and that's why I go to recovery meetings. To surround myself with encouraging and successful people.

It doesn't matter if you are currently successful in life right now or not, because "Even Though" you may be going through a hard time, you were once successful before addiction took over and destroyed your life. And that's what really matters, because it shows you have the potential to be successful again. And your life, and your story and experiences, well they do matter. Do we want to keep doing the same thing over and over again? No, we want to take the information that we learn from other people who have lived through and survived addiction, and use their stories to actually make a difference and bring change. If you want change in this world, then be that change and inspire people to want to change. We need to show them the way. It all starts and ends with us. Be the light for people in this dark world, like a window in a dark room.

Addiction is a silent killer and a professional thief. It will rob you blind and steal everything from you that you have ever loved, and then it will try to take your life. But be careful, because sometimes it will take your life first before it takes anything else at all. Addiction is after the heart and soul. As it slowly starts to take our life and consume our soul, it breaks the hearts of our loved ones as they stand by watching helplessly, knowing there is nothing they can do, until *you* decide, that *you* want to help yourself.

I was recently thinking about how I could try to explain what it feels like to be an addict stuck in active addiction to someone that has never had addiction issues. This is the best comparison I could think of: Have you ever had that feeling when you wake up from a scary dream, and it felt so real that you start breathing really heavy and have like an immediate anxiety attack, but then you normally calm down after a few seconds? Well, imagine what it would be like if you didn't calm down, and you stayed in that panic state of mind. That's what it's like every day waking up being addicted to opioids without a prescription. You immediately start to freak out about how you are going to find some more, so that you don't get sick. It's like you are not even living to live, you are living to get high, which is really not even living at all. Your judgment is clouded, and you can't think clearly, and all of your decisions are influenced by your addiction. We lose the ability to think for ourselves, and it's hard to know what's wrong and what's right when our moral compass is off. If you are being guided in life by your addiction rather than your morals, then you are most certainly heading down an inevitable path of destruction, and it's just a matter of time.

When someone is in active addiction, their thought process is just so much different than that of an average person. It doesn't matter if you beg an addict, or if you plead with them, or if you try and bribe them, or even if you try and lock them in a cage. It still will not change their mind. The only way that an addict will get clean and get into recovery is if *they* decide that *they* want to change.

For those who do end up going to jail and then getting released, it's a race to who gets to you first, your family and friends who want to help you and get you into a treatment program, or the drug dealer. The reason for this is that, while you are in jail and withdrawing from your drug of choice, all you think about is getting high and getting well. You even dream about it.

When I was in jail, I had some crazy, intense hallucinations and like drug-fueled flashbacks of being on the outside and getting high every night. The hold that these opioids have on people nowadays is so strong, both physically and mentally, that it's honestly like you are being possessed. It doesn't matter what you have to do, you're going to do it, regardless of the conse-quences, to make sure that the addiction gets fed. Inside the addicted mind, there is nothing more important. People who are addicted to opioids, them not having their drugs is like them not having air to breathe, and getting dope-sick and going through that withdrawal is their biggest fear. That's what addiction is: You give up everything for that one thing. But that is also the beauty of recovery, because you can give up that one thing and get everything back.

We need more treatment facilities, and we need to have these beds ready and open for addicts who are brave enough to admit they have a problem and need help. We must get them that help when they need it, not forty-five days later like they did to one of my best friends, Zach. He knew he had a problem, and was brave enough to ask for help. But he was told the best they could do was forty-five days out until they could get him into a bed. Well, guess what? He didn't even make it five days. We as a society failed him. And we can and must do better. You build it, and I promise you, they will come.

Addicts are their own harshest critics, this I can guarantee you, and anything that you tell us, believe me, we have already beat ourselves up a dozen times over it. Instead of crushing ourselves, we must pick ourselves up as well, and that starts with how we feel about ourselves. Instead of saying, wow, I look ugly, we should tell ourselves that we are beautiful. It's possible to be confident without being conceded. Instead of telling ourselves we are weak, we should remind ourselves of just how strong we are, and how much we have had to overcome to get to where we are today. Instead of telling ourselves no, I can't do this; tell yourself, that hell yes, I can do this, because you can get through anything, no matter the situation.

And always remember that God will never give us more than we can handle. Now, He may push us and test us to our absolute limits, but he will never set us up for failure. To those in recovery, you are absolutely amazing in your own way, and you should stop doubting yourself, because you are without a doubt an inspiration to people who are still struggling with their addiction and would give anything to be where you are today. You are alive, you are here today, and you are able and capable of being that beacon of hope for those who need it the most.

Every single person in long-term recovery is so much more important than they even know. It is up to us to show others that it is possible to beat addiction and get our lives back. We can do this by sharing our stories and experiences with each other. There are so many people who go through addiction, get clean, and go into recovery, but then never talk about it, which is okay. But the more people who share their stories, the better. Each story is proof that addiction is treatable, no matter how severe.

Addiction comes in all kinds of shapes and sizes. It doesn't discriminate and will gladly destroy any family it can, just like it did to mine. All those sleepless nights my family spent worrying and wondering if I was dead, or hurt, and were just waiting for a phone call to confirm their worst fears. Luckily, that call never came. But I can only imagine how awful that must have been, and for that I do genuinely apologize.

I went to jail for jay-walking and drug paraphernalia. When I got out of jail in Phoenix, I was in a city that I did not know, around people that I did not know, and I was lost and scared. I didn't know what to do. This disease will gladly take any life it can. It's pure evil and we never know who it's affecting, because "Even Though" some people are open and honest about their struggles with addiction, many are silent and remain isolated, too embarrassed to ask for help. Or they are scared or worried what others might think about them.

I truly do believe that the Devil does exist, and that this evil addiction is his disease, and this opioid epidemic is how he is spreading his "medicine" for his disease. For anyone who doesn't believe in God, or the Devil, that is fine. I would never preach religion on anyone. The reason I hear most often though is because you can't physically see them, so therefore there is no proof that they do actually exist. To that, I say to you this: To me, God is like love; I can't see it, but I can feel it. And the Devil is real, and once he gets you hooked on his "medicine," you become a slave to the disease of addiction that he created.

To escape his grasp and to fight back, you must go through at least three to five days of hell, withdrawing, just to get back to your normal world. Oftentimes, it's even longer than that. I myself have made this trip through hell and back multiple times, and each time escaping the Devil's grasp became increasingly more difficult. Especially this last and final time. I didn't think I was going to make it. I was unconscious and unresponsive for over four hours. That was my rock bottom, but somehow, some way, I pulled through. I spent the next five days in the hospital, before I had to be taken back to jail. When I woke up in the hospital, the doctor said, "Welcome back sir, we thought we had lost you."

As I began to regain consciousness, I started to vomit, and then I realized I had been given Narcan (Naloxone), through my IV. Suddenly, I began to shiver as I felt a cold chill starting to run down the back of my spine. I started to get so cold, like colder than I have ever been in my entire life. It was like all of the blood in my body was frozen, and like I had ice in my veins. I couldn't even sit up and move, because both of my wrists were handcuffed to the bed. I felt so helpless. There was nothing else I could do besides bow my head and start to cry. I couldn't even wipe the tears off that were running down my face. The totality of the situation hit me all at once, and it was a very overwhelming feeling. In that moment, I don't even know what bothered me more: the fact that I was in police custody, and had no more drugs, and was about to go through a withdrawal, or the fact that I pretty much just died and had to be brought back to life. That gives you a glimpse into what my mindset was like back then, and just how important the drugs were to me.

That may sound absolutely crazy to someone who has never dealt with addiction, or seen someone they love have to go through a withdrawal. For those who don't know how bad the withdrawal from opioids or painkillers or Fentanyl or even alcohol is, let me try to explain it to you. Imagine feeling sick, like sicker than you have ever felt. So weak you can't even stand up or walk because your legs are shaking so bad. Your nose starts to run, then you start to sweat, then comes the cold sweats, followed by the hot and cold chills. As soon as you feel cold and start to warm up, you then start to feel hot and need to cool down. Your joints start to hurt, your muscles start to cramp, and your bones start to ache. You get nauseous and throw up. Next thing you know you got the runs, and it's coming out both ends. You don't know what to do, you start to get a headache from thinking about it so much, then that turns into a migraine, and then your mind tricks you into thinking that the only way to feel better is by giving in and taking whatever you are addicted to. This could literally and absolutely kill you if not taken seriously and treated properly.

Five days later, right when I was about to be unhooked from all the machines and discharged from the hospital, the nurse who was unhooking me asked if I was okay. I just kind of sat there for a second. Then all kinds of emotions hit me, and I started to get tears in my eyes. I said, "No, not really. I'm scared." She said,

"What are you scared about?" I said, "I'm scared of the uncertainty of what's going to happen, and I have to go back to jail and I might be in there for a long time, and I'm also scared about getting clean and staying off of the drugs, like I don't know if I can do that, or if I'm even strong enough." Then I said, "I really just don't know if I'm going to be able to make it through this or not. She looked at me and said, "Can I ask you a question?" I said, "Sure." She said, "Do you believe in God?" I looked up, looked her right in the eye, and said, "Yes, I do." She gave me a huge smile and said, "Then you have nothing to worry about, because God has your back, and He will never abandon you in your time of need, if you truly need him." I then looked at her arm, and she had one of my favorite bible verses tatted. It said, "This too shall pass." When I saw that, I really started to get emotional, because I knew she was right about God, and in that moment when I felt so lonely and scared, I now felt a sense of comfort and peace in knowing that I wouldn't be going through this alone. That message of "This too shall pass" is what helped me get through those tough first few weeks. And it's still something I tell myself to this day whenever life gets tough. We walk by faith, not by sight.

My dad used to always ask me if I had a drug problem, and if I was an addict, and tell me that addiction is a disease that runs in our blood. I used to just blow him off and would do what addicts do. I would lie, and I would go to great lengths to try to "hide everything." But really, who was I kidding? I used to think I was so good at hiding my addiction and that I was so smooth and sneaky, but in reality it was blatantly obvious to everyone around me. The only person I was really fooling was myself.

I'm now three and a half years clean, and in long term recovery, and I share my story all the time. But it wasn't like that in the beginning. It took almost six months for me to open up and feel comfortable enough to share that dark, lonely part of my life with people, especially around people I didn't know. But I came to realize that the recovery community is like one big, giant family and the support the recovery community provides to people is so important.

Before I felt comfortable enough to share it with the people in my recovery meetings, I wrote all my memories of pain, and hurt, and sadness, and trauma, including being homeless on the streets and nearly freezing to death as an addict. I told the paper all of that, because I didn't feel comfortable enough telling that to another person. I have now come to realize just how therapeutic writing has been for me. It has given me an outlet to share things I needed to get off my chest but that I wasn't quite ready to share with anyone else just yet. I am no longer ashamed or embarrassed to talk about the person that I once was and the experiences and struggles that I went through, because it helped me become the person that I am today. I have been humbled and have gone through some real humility and I wouldn't trade the perspective and appreciation I have for life now, for anything. I'm just so grateful to be alive and to be able to share my story and change the narrative, and be able to tell my story myself, instead of having my story told by someone else at my funeral. I have lost many friends to this addiction, and they will never get the chance to tell their own story. That's why I want to try to make a difference for all of those people who never got the chance too, and are now, forever silent.

When people hear my story, the question I get asked the most is: What is the biggest difference I have noticed in my life from when I was out using on the streets, compared to the three and a half years clean I now have under my belt? To answer that question, I think the best way to explain it would be to think about the senses we have as humans. Specifically, three of the senses: sight, hearing, and touch or feel. While I was using and homeless on the streets, I almost always felt invisible. It was like nobody saw me, and, honestly, like nobody cared. There were many times I would cry and get emotional when I felt nobody was around, because one thing that I learned from jail was to not show emotion around people because they would think I was weak, and would try to pick on me, or punk me. So I took that same angry, tough mentality onto the streets with me. Most of the time I would be crying is because I was dealing with a mental health episode. You see, I'm a person who suffers from extreme anxiety. And doing all of those different drugs I was doing was making me paranoid and was making my anxiety a million times worse. I was literally having a mental breakdown and a panic attack at the same time, almost hyperventilating and just shaking and rocking back and forth. And people would just walk by and look at me, and either laugh or just keep walking by and not say a word.

After they would walk by, I would think to myself: Wow, do I not matter? Or am I dirty and ugly? Or does the way I look just scare people? Or, am I just that much of a piece of shit? It literally was like being a ghost, people never stopping to ask, "Hey, are you okay?" Or, "Do you need some help? After having so many people walk by me day after day, week after week, month after month, never having a care in the world about me, after being ignored for so long, one day I actually started weeping. I made it loud, so that there was no way that people couldn't hear me, because I had been thinking to myself: Well, maybe, I'm just too quiet, so they can't hear me and that's why they don't see me.

After crying and weeping louder and louder, just begging for someone to stop and acknowledge me and ask how I was, and if I was okay, and if I needed anything, or if I needed someone to talk to, or just tell me that I wasn't alone and that I did matter, and that somebody did care about me. And hoping maybe, just maybe, someone was going to stop and pick me up off of the ground, give me a hug, and tell me that everything was going to be okay. To tell you the truth though, that's not what happened, because this is not a fairytale, this is my life, and the world can be a very cruel place. What actually happened next was, the first guy who stopped to "check on me," walked by and kicked my shoes and said, "Stop crying, you little crybaby bitch," and threw a full can of soda at me. It hit me in the head, and gave me a real good cut that started gushing blood over my right eye.

Immediately, my mind switched back to that jail mentality, and I went from crying and sad to straight pissed off, just like that. I went to stand up to confront the guy, and it was like someone was holding me down and did not want me to get up. I finally got about halfway back to my feet, and then I suddenly lost my balance. It was like somebody pushed me and said, "No, just stay down. It's not worth it."

Then I thought to myself, *When is enough, enough? And when is the hate and anger going to end?* I told myself it ends right now, and that I was done spreading hate and always being angry, and I just wanted to be happy for once; and spread love and kindness to each person that I met. I told myself, *I'm done with this lifestyle and I'm not going to keep hurting myself anymore.*

What happened next was kind of a blur, but someone finally

did stop and help me. They helped me to my feet, walked me to a nearby CVS store, and went inside and bought me some food, water, and some first aid stuff to clean all the blood off me. Once I got cleaned up, I went to the back side of CVS, sat down, drank my water, and ate my food. Then I guess I must have passed out, because wouldn't you know it? The next thing I remember was being woken up by the police and getting taken to jail. I had a warrant for missing court. When you are homeless, time is kind of irrelevant. I never really knew the date or what day of the week it was, unless someone mentioned it.

Upon getting released from jail that time, I finally got into a treatment program called Bicycle Health. It was an intensive outpatient program done via telehealth. I was able to attend all my doctor appointments virtually on Zoom, and all of the recovery meetings are done that way as well. I could do everything online from the comfort of my own house. If it wasn't for that program, I wouldn't be here today. It truly did save my life, and that's how my current journey into recovery got started. I am still currently enrolled in that program, to keep myself accountable. It has been a great support system for me and an outlet for things that I needed to talk about when I didn't know who else to talk to.

No matter how many times I got sent to jail, it never actually got me clean and off the drugs. But the first time I got into a treatment program, I got clean, relapsed one time, stayed with the same program, and am still going strong! To me, this is proof that treatment programs do work, and, when it comes to addiction, incarceration is not rehabilitation. Jail will not rehabilitate you, but a treatment program could.

I know what it feels like to be treated badly, and have people be rude to you, and have your feelings hurt, and be made fun of, and be bullied, and belittled. And it didn't feel good. During some later self-reflection I realized that, in the past, I used to be that person who made people feel that way. I guess you could say that things came full circle, and that I got a big dose of karma. I would like to sincerely apologize to anyone I may have ever done that to, or hurt their feelings in any way!

I was attacked, robbed, jumped, beaten, extorted, pistol whipped, sexually assaulted, and humiliated many different times while homeless on the streets. After being homeless for about a year, I was so frail, weak, malnourished, and sick, that I honestly got punked by pretty much everyone. I was just like a walking corpse, like I couldn't even fight back if I tried. It was like I lost the ability to defend myself, which is crazy, because I was a captain of my varsity wrestling team and used to train MMA. But I had no energy, and no strength to do anything, besides get high and lay there like the worthless shell of a man that I had become. The drugs and the lack of food were draining what little living part of me I had left. The other addicts around me were just swarming like vultures, waiting for me to drop and die, so they could take whatever I had off my lifeless body. I watched someone overdose and die, in the war zone in Albuquerque, and then saw people run up and rob his dead body before the cops got there.

Now that I know what all of that felt like, I never want to make someone else feel how I felt. That's why I share my story with everyone, to bring awareness, so that hopefully someone else doesn't have to go through what I went through and repeat the same mistakes I made, and that they can use my story as a guide of what NOT to do in life.

When I see someone going through a similar struggle that I went through, I genuinely feel for that person on such a deep and personal level, because I know that pain firsthand, and I can't help but feel some sympathy and empathy for them. We may think we know how things in life are going to turn out, but we never really know for sure, because reality is the killer of expectations. We may have high hopes, huge dreams, and big expectations of how we want things to go, but more often than not, reality does not live up to the expectations that we had in our mind. That's why the saying goes, "Hope for the best, but expect the worst," because if we expect something to happen, and it doesn't, that can honestly be really disappointing and can lead to some dark places.

When I was eighteen months into recovery, I wrote this: Eighteen months of sobriety, after eighteen years of addiction of every variety. Recovery is not just a choice, it is a mindset. You have to change the way you think. You have to make a conscious decision that you want to change your life for the better. To truly be successful in your recovery, you have to be all in. You cannot half-ass it or be on the fence about your decision; perception is reality.

When I think back about being homeless, the only good thing I can remember was feeling like I was free. I had no responsibilities, and I could go wherever I wanted to, whenever I wanted to. That was my perception of reality. But now, looking back on it, oh how wrong I was! I was never really free. I was a prisoner in my own personal prison, and a slave in my own version of hell. I was a servant and the drugs were my master; my mind had been hijacked.

They say that our eyes are windows into our soul, but when I would look in the mirror at my reflection, it was like my soul was gone, like the window had been closed and covered with a dark sheet. It was like my eyes were a hollow black shell of emptiness, inside of my dilated pupils. I would spend all day, every day, getting high, and if I wasn't doing that, then I was scheming and thinking to myself how I could earn some money to buy some more drugs. That is the entirety of what my life had become: buy drugs, do drugs, repeat. That is what my life consisted of. I didn't care about anything else, or anyone else. Honestly, I didn't even care about myself. I couldn't even think for myself anymore, because that power had been taken away from me by my addiction. I was helpless and had a problem, and my master deceived me and said, "Drugs were the solution."

Everyone who actually cared about me was worried and was looking for me, because I had been missing. But the truth is, I was lost and didn't want to be found. I had been gone so long, and I was so lost, that I forgot what it felt like to feel things. I used to get high to try to forget about all of my problems, and try to numb all of my pain. But I started to become numb to everything, even things I didn't want to become numb to. So much so, that I forgot what it felt like to smile, to laugh, to feel happy or safe. I forgot there were good people and good things in this world, because I was always surrounded by bad. I felt like I was worthless and that my life was over. It was like all of my hopes and dreams had been shattered, like broken glass when it's cold. I couldn't function or do anything for myself, without having my master around to pull the strings on the puppet that I had become.

It was like I had a death wish, always trying to chase the thing that could kill me. But that's what my body craved. I felt like I would die without it, but doing too much could be fatal as well. You never know what you would do until you are backed into a corner with nothing, because you go into survival mode. It's like there is no more right or wrong at that point. It's either you do it, or you die, and if you do it, you might die anyway. I would just like to tell my former puppet master this: There was a time that I was so reliant and dependent on you that I would have done anything to please you, because you meant everything to me. Which is ironic, because now you mean nothing to me, because you are nothing. I literally created you out of thin air; without me you cease to exist. There is no addiction if there is no addict there to feed it.

Recovery isn't about just going back to the person we were before our addiction; it's about becoming a wiser, and stronger, and more humble version of ourselves. I am beyond grateful for the fresh outlook I have on life, and "Even Though" there are so many things I want to go do now that I'm clean and in long term recovery, I'm much more cautious than I used to be, and I now take a much more measured approach to life in general. Because I know that a relapse would be a death sentence for me. My body has already been through so much over the years, and I now have some serious health problems because of it. In the last two and a half years, I have been put to sleep thirteen times to have an endoscopy procedure done to try to expand the diameter of my digestive tract because I have something called a "stricture." Which I had to do because I couldn't swallow at all and my medication and food kept getting stuck in my throat and I felt like I was choking. I have since been put on a new medication called Dupixent, and it has completely changed my quality of life in such an amazing way. And I'm so happy to say that I am almost in remission now. I couldn't swallow, so I had to shred all of my food in a food processor, like a baby. I was so skinny and weak and had no energy. I used to never even really leave my house. Right now, I feel stronger than I have ever felt before in my entire life. I know I will still have some of those health problems though for the rest of my life. It's just like addiction, it never goes away, like you never stop being an addict or grow out of it. It will always be there, just waiting for us to mess up and feed it. To me addiction is like a volcano. It may never erupt again. But it is lying there dormant inside of us just hoping for a moment of weakness. You can manage your addiction for the rest of your life and live in recovery without having any slip ups; but it never goes away.

We learn tools in recovery that teach us what our triggers are and learn coping mechanisms to help with any urges or temptations to use that we might have. It is natural to have thoughts of using, and it's okay if we get urges or cravings, because that is the addict in us. But there is the difference between active addiction and long-term recovery. In active addiction, you act on those impulses. In recovery, you remove those impulses by replacing that thought with something else. Until the pain of your addiction is greater than the pain of your recovery, you will stay addicted. We cannot feel joy if we refuse to feel pain. Painkillers do not help when the only pain that you are killing is yourself.

The only thing as good as a success story is a story of redemption, because a redemption story is about someone who already was that success story but had a fall from grace. Or, in my case, a nose dive all the way to the bottom where the rocks lay a-broken from all of the shattered hopes and dreams that go to die at rocks bottom. Because, truthfully, if you are an addict, and you hit rock bottom, then chances are you are not far from death, because the only way to get lower than the rocks is if you're in the dirt.

So, there I was at rock bottom, not far from death's doorstep. Honestly, just on the other side of the valley of the shadow of death. Sure, I was scared, and yeah, I could have just withered away and slowly died out there at rock bottom. But I didn't. Instead, I was gazing out and looking around at the world my addiction had torn down, thinking to myself, *Is this the way my story ends?* Then off in the distance I heard a boom. I quickly reached down and picked up one of those broken rocks for protection, and I saw something move. So I threw my little rock out into the black abyss, out of fear. I was expecting to see a black cloud of death, but that's not what it was. From afar it was like a light and a vision slowly becoming brighter and brighter, and clearer, until suddenly, I saw it. It was a phoenix being reborn through the ashes. And I realized I was like that phoenix, and I too wanted to be reborn through the ashes—the ashes of my failures, and the ashes of my mistakes, the ashes of my shortcomings, and my lies, and the ashes, the ashes of me being a bad person. Because, you know what? I may have burned my whole world to the ground, and hurting my family and breaking their trust is something that tears at my heartstrings. But "Even Though" I burnt the good things in my life to the ground, I was also burning all the negative things in that world.

When I think about all the negative things I burnt down, people, places, and habits is what comes to my mind. When it comes to people, I had to completely change the "friends" I was hanging out with. Tell me who your friends are, and I will tell you who you are. Everyone around me was getting high, and was an addict. So what did I do? I got high, and I was an addict. The craziest part, though, was that most of the people I would be around, I had nothing in common with them besides the drugs. I started to slowly change out my friend group during active addiction. I didn't mean to, and it wasn't on purpose. I knew my real friends would not condone me getting high around them, so I hate to say it, but I started to isolate from them just so that I could get high and wouldn't have to listen to them voice their concerns about what I was doing. I have completely changed my friend group in my life today. The friends and people that I choose to surround myself with are good people and have high character, and if they don't, then I don't need them in my life. I wasted way too much time on people that didn't matter, and did nothing but drag me down, and they were the what have you done for me lately type of friends. I'm sorry but if you have to constantly do things for people just to be their friend, then chances are they probably are not really your friend. Being there for someone when they really need you, that's what a real friend is. If you have to always prove yourself just to be someone's friend; is it really even worth it? Your friends are a direct reflection of yourself, so be careful who you call a friend. Most people in our lives are just acquaintances

When it comes to places, I learned that I had to change my surroundings and my environment. If you just keep going back to the same place that you were while you were using, around people that are still using, then you are just asking for trouble and are playing with fire, and it could be very easy to have a slip up. I know I have an addictive personality so the more precaution I can take to set boundaries, the better chance of staying clean I have! I would get arrested and then released and then would go right back to the same area, and the same hood, get arrested again and start the whole process over. It is a vicious cycle and if you don't get out of it, then you will stay stuck in it. If you stay stuck in the fast money drug world, it only ends one of two ways: in a jail cell or a body bag. I moved from Albuquerque to Phoenix to change my environment, because if I kept going back to the same area, around the same people, and the same places that I used to, it was going to kill me.

Habits is the final thing that I feel I burnt down in that world. I used to think getting high was the answer to every single problem in my life. At the time it seemed like the solution. Little did I know, it was just adding on to the problems. Multiplying the problems may be the more accurate term. It made everything in my life so much worse. I wasn't ever actually addressing the issue, I was just numbing myself hoping the problem would pass. When I get sad now, and if I'm having a hard time, instead of isolating and trying to deal with all of my problems myself, I reach out and talk about it. Most of the time, I feel way better after I get it off my chest, and they give me advice that I wouldn't have thought of myself. The opposite of addiction is connection. I have found much healthier ways to cope with things when I'm having a tough time. Instead of turning to those harmful habits, I now have habits that aren't going to hurt me. I go to the gym, I do push-ups, I go for walks, I play kickball, I write and journal, I listen to music, I go to recovery meetings, I go to Celebrate Recovery, I talk about my problems to my friends and family. I am not alone, and none of us are. If you really don't have anyone else, you still always have God. I never knew he was all I needed, until He was all I had.

It is up to us, though, if we decide to share and let people in who care about us.

I moved to Phoenix for a fresh start, and like the city I live in, I too want to be reborn with three solid roots to grow from: One, earning my family's trust back. Two, having integrity and doing the right thing, even if nobody is watching—shit, especially if nobody is watching. Three, hopefully one day I will not only think of myself as a good person, but other people will view me as a good person as well. It's not that I was a bad person, I was just doing a lot of evil stuff guided by my addiction. It caused a whole lot of damage in my life, so now I'm just trying to repair as much as I possibly can.

I still have a long way to go, but I feel I'm well on my way and heading in the right direction on this journey. Actually, I guess you could say I'm on my redemption tour, trying to redeem myself, and make amends, and make right with the people who I hurt the most, but who also mean the most to me. When life is going well, everyone wants to be your friend and say they are there for you. But only when life gets rough will you find out who is truly there for you, and honestly not to sugarcoat it, but you find out who actually gives a shit about you. And, for me, that's family. Blood is thicker than water. They were the only ones there for me, no matter how many times I made mistakes, and believe me, it was a ridiculous amount. But still no matter how badly I screwed up, they still never turned their backs on me, when many other "friends" had.

But you know what? At some point we need to stop caring what other people think about us, and start focusing on how we feel about ourselves. Instead of tearing each other down, we must pick each other up. The world will already try to tear us down and beat us up. We don't need to do it too ourselves or each other! You are not your thoughts. Thoughts are like feelings, which are like the wind, they come and they go. You are your actions, and decisions. I used to really struggle with depression, and I still do from time to time. I get in these ruts, where my mood is really down and I don't want to do anything. It can be very hard to pull myself out of it sometimes. But that's another example of a perfect time to ask for help. I used to be in a depressed state of mind for weeks, sometimes even months at a time. I would keep everything bottled up and to myself and would drive myself crazy with all my thoughts. There was no one to talk to or at least no one around that I wanted to talk to at the time.

But now when I feel myself starting to slide back into depression, I catch myself trying to isolate and push away the people that care about me. I normally recognize it after a day or two, but sometimes it can go on a little longer before I notice what I'm doing. When I do realize I'm starting to do that, I know that I need to reach out to friends or family and let them be that support system for me.

Depression can be crippling if you let it control you. Even if your decisions are influenced slightly because of depression, it can have a drastic impact on your daily life. It may start out slow and small. But if not taken seriously, it will keep growing and spreading and start to affect every part of your life. Depression is like cancer; there is nothing good about it.

Some of the best advice I have received while in recovery was that, if you have something on your mind, you should talk about it. Holding it in only hurts ourselves. And if you have no one to talk to, and you're struggling, then go ahead and cry and let it out. It is okay to cry. I promise you that crying does not make you weak, it shows you have real actual feelings. And honestly it just means you're a human being like everybody else.

When you go through something in life that absolutely breaks you to your core, but doesn't kill you, it really truly does make you stronger. Trauma can happen in seconds but can be lived out through a lifetime. If you have ever been hurt before, but you are healed now, then you now have the power to help heal those who are still hurting. Going through something traumatic can really put life in perspective for you, too, and make you realize what, and also who, is actually important.

For me, staying sober from what I was addicted to is important. And I now have all of the love and support in the world from my family. I finally opened up to them about my struggle with addiction, and now I finally feel seen. I also feel I have found my voice as a writer, so now I feel heard.

And as far as feel and touch is concerned, my family gives me all of the hugs I could ever want, and even sometimes when I don't want them. I truly do believe that the girl of my dreams does exist; but we just haven't met yet. I haven't dated anyone for a long time, because my thought process was: If I can't even take care of myself, then how can I expect to take care of someone else? I also needed to learn how to love myself again before I could love someone else.

And "Even Though" it is okay to plan and think of the future, we must live in the now, and in the present. If we don't, then life will surely pass us by. It's not too late to get your life back, no matter who you are or how bad of a situation you may be in. It's not too late, unless you give up and quit fighting, or until you die, you still have a chance to live the life that you want to live.

Now do we get to decide when and how we die? Probably not. But we can choose the way that we live, until the day that we die. I have lived with and battled addiction most of my adult life, and I have been through hell and back. So believe me when I say I know what you are going through. And just know that I hear you, I see you, and I feel you, because, in a way, I am you, and you are me. As different and unique as each of our stories in life are, our stories and our paths into recovery are so similar.

I have a message for anyone who ever hears this. To the women: You are enough, you are beautiful, and you do matter. Know your worth and stop giving people discounts. And to the fellas, to the fellas, I say unto you this: You are handsome and good looking in your own way, and "Even Though" your outer appearance may not be the best, just know that on some real talk, your inner beauty can outshine any flaws you may have on your outer appearance. Because always remember it does not cost you anything to be kind to people, and unlike trust that must be earned, respect is a must and should be given to people at all times. And I promise you that if you treat each person you meet in your life with absolute respect and kindness, people will see you for who you truly are as a person, and that inner beauty will radiate from you. If the world was like the movie "Shallow Hal," where you only saw what people looked like based off the person that they were on the inside, the world would be a much better place because then you would have to actually be a good person in order to be considered beautiful, and you couldn't just hide behind good looks.

I really do try so hard nowadays to get to know people for

who they are on the inside, and what type of character they have as a person, rather than judging them off of their outer appearance and making assumptions about who they are as a person based off how they look. I have to remind myself that no matter how someone looks today, that all of our looks are going to eventually fade, but a beautiful soul will not.

I used to have this false misconception that walking around pissed off all the time and being rude to people made me seem tough, and made people respect me. But I was wrong. It's the opposite of that, really. People don't respect you just because you walk around with an attitude all the time. You get respect by giving respect. Be kind to people, and treat them well, and good things will happen in your life. To some people, respect means even more to them than money. To this day, I still choose to continue to spread love, not hate.

Finally, I will leave you with this: If we can switch our mentality from I'm broken and helpless to I'm growing and healing, watch how fast your life can change. Use your experiences to make a difference in this world. Experience is priceless, because experience is the hardest kind of teacher. It gives you the test first and the lesson later. Please use those hard lessons we have all learned to hopefully help prevent other people from having to go through what we went through. I'm a big believer in that we grow through what we go through. The legendary artist Pablo Picasso has a famous quote that says, "The meaning of life is to find your gift. The purpose of life is to give it away." Now, we have all heard of the golden rule: Treat others how you want to be treated. Well, we should treat everyone with the upmost respect, until we are disrespected, and it shouldn't matter who they are. Shouldn't matter if it is a friend, or a foe, or a cop, or your bro, they should all be treated Even… Though.

Dedicated to Zach

Earlier in the book, I talked about losing one of my best friends to an overdose. His name was Zach Montoya. He was only 28 years old and still had his entire life ahead of him. Zach, I wish I would have known that the last time I saw you was the last time that I would ever see you. I think about it frequently. I can't help but wonder what I might have said to you. It probably would have been something like this: Thank you for being my friend.

I moved to Los Alamos, NM, from Idaho Falls, ID, when I was 12. I was good at sports, but I was cocky and full of myself and was extremely rude to people, so, needless to say, I didn't have a whole lot of friends. Zach would be rude right back to me and would make fun of me. That's honestly probably why we got along so well. LOL. We met playing football in middle school. I was in 7th grade and he was in 8th grade. I was good enough to play up on the 8th grade team which is probably the only reason he tolerated having me around. I was like that little annoying kid that hung around who had a squeaky voice because my balls hadn't dropped yet.

When I got to high school, it was rough. I lost my friend group and none of my older football friends wanted to hang out with me, because no upper classmen wanted to be seen with a little loser freshman. So I became a loner. I started drinking alcohol during freshman year, and got arrested for a minor in possession of alcohol. I got kicked off the football team, so I started to play on the golf team instead. I didn't think I was going to know anyone on there, but lo and behold it was my old pal Zach. I'm not going to lie; I was probably a whole lot more excited to see him than he was to see me.

I was kind of like his secret friend, I feel like. We would always have fun playing golf and messing around putting and chipping at the course, but as soon as we were back at school, we would act like we didn't really even know each other. It did hurt my feelings a little bit, but, honestly, I was just happy to have a friend. I didn't want to tarnish his reputation by him being seen with me. He was always a pretty popular guy; everyone always seemed to love him, both older and younger peers.

Zach was goofy as hell! He had one of those laughs that was infectious. He would start to crack up about something, and then everybody would start laughing. He definitely lit up every room he walked into.

I used to bug Zach so much about taking me up to a mountain party so I could try to seem cool and party with all the older kids. Where we went to high school at, it was a very small town with less than 15,000 people. There was literally nothing to do for the kids in our town, so we would go up into the Jemez Mountains and get drunk and smoke weed and cigarettes. I would say that we all thought we were so cool, but honestly we just wanted to have fun and find a way to relieve some stress because our school was one of the hardest in the country. It put a lot of pressure on the students, and a lot of us did not handle that very well.

Zach and I did become real good friends during my junior year. We both played varsity golf and would have a freaking blast on the overnight golf tournament trips. Zach graduated in 2008, and went off to college at NM State University in Las Cruces, NM.

During my senior year, in 2009, I was a freaking mess and was honestly lucky to even graduate. I was drinking, smoking, popping pills, snorting Oxys, doing lines of cocaine. As soon as I graduated, I packed all my stuff up at my parents' house and moved down to Albuquerque the next day. Life went downhill pretty quickly for me after that.

Four months later, I was arrested for the first time as an adult on drug-related charges. I was on unsupervised probation for six months. During that time, I moved back to my parents' house by Los Alamos. As soon as I completed probation and was "free," I went right back to using painkillers.

It had been a couple years since I had seen Zach. At the end of 2010, I went to Denver, CO, for a New Year's Eve rave called Decadence. I ran into Zach there and he told me to come hang out with him after the event ended. I went up to his hotel room, and after about 5 minutes or so, Zach pulled me to the side and proceeded to tell me that he had started doing Oxy and asked if I knew where to get any. I just so happened to be hooked on the same thing he was, so pretty much every time I saw him after that, we would end up getting high together.

I saw Zach at a whole bunch of festivals that year. About six months later, I went back to Denver to go to the Global Dance Festival at Red Rocks Amphitheatre. It was two days long, and it was so much freaking fun! Zach and I, and a bunch of our old high school friends were there, and it was just a great time seeing everyone again and just enjoying life and each other's company.

About two months later, pretty much our entire friend group that we saw in Denver came out to Las Vegas and went to the first ever EDC (Electric Daisy Carnival) Vegas. It was at the Las Vegas Motor Speedway where NASCAR races. It was on the track and literally took up the entire venue. There were over 175,000 people there. It was three days long and went from dusk till dawn, 6 p.m. to 6 a.m. each day.

I saw Zach here and there the first couple of days. On the third and final day, there was a DJ called Stanton Warriors who we both really wanted to see. The only problem though was that everyone in our group was just flat out exhausted from all of the walking and they didn't want to go until like 11 p.m., and Stanton Warriors came on at 7 p.m. So Zach and I decided to head over there early, just me and him, to catch their set. It was honestly amazing and was definitely worth getting there early, even if we were tired. We hung out the entire night, and to this day, it was maybe the best and most fun night that I can ever remember. Like if there is such a thing as the best night ever, where the world just stops around you and you just live in the moment, that was it. I don't know if I have ever smiled so much, danced so hard, or head banged until my neck hurt so much. It was just the perfect night! From the stages to the people, to the performers, the music was unbelievable.

We saw this DJ group called Mt. Eden who was from New Zealand. It was their first ever performance in the United States, and they played all their best songs in the original versions, and it was just the most incredible set that either of us had ever heard.

Later that night, I walked by a merchandise stand and they had a shirt that said Mt. Eden is Meds. I ended up buying that shirt because their music and set that I just heard was literally like medicine for my soul. The bass was so heavy it would like rattle your entire body and would like move you from side to side as the crowd swayed together.

The music was great, it wasn't even like you heard it, more so, like you felt it. Then a fireworks show started. It was the best fireworks show I have ever seen. It was like a grand finale for about an hour straight. With all of these amazing things going on around us, the best part though was the fact that I was there with my best friend, and got to make memories, and have an experience that I will never forget and will truly cherish for the rest of my life.

In 2012, just nine months later, I got in some big trouble. I ended up catching felony drug charges and landed in federal custody of the U.S. Marshals. My life changed forever after that day. After a little while, I was later released on pre-trial into the custody of my parents. Had I gone on the run, my parents would have been held criminally responsible for me. The feds do not play! After being on pre-trial for 13 months, I took a plea and was sentenced to three years' probation.

I got a good job and worked my way up through the company and stayed out of trouble for almost 10 years until 2020. In 2014, it had been almost four years since I had seen Zach. He came into my work. I was a deli manager at the time at our local grocery store. He told me that he was living with his mom in town and that he was working up at the golf course. I was freaking stoked when he told me that because I made my own schedule, so I would go in at like 5:30 a.m. and be off by about 2:30 p.m. every day, and then I could play golf in the afternoons.

Since I was on federal probation, I wasn't messing around at all because I was on a zero tolerance waiver from the judge, meaning one slip up and I wasn't going to be seen again in public for a long time. In other words, I had some serious prison time hanging over my head. The fear of being locked up for years was a great motivator to stay out of trouble. I was looking at up to 20 years on a maximum sentence.

I bought a season pass at the local golf course where Zach worked. We played golf together that year, I believe, like 135 times. Those are memories that I will always hold onto. He was definitely my golfing buddy. I used to always see Zach and his grandpa at the course. They were extremely close and played together all the time.

In 2015, I got promoted at my job and moved to Santa Fe, NM. But in 2017, I started to do painkillers again to get me through the labor intensive job that I was doing. That quickly spiraled out of control and I ended up losing my job and started getting deep back into the drug world.

In 2018, I ran into Zach again. It had been almost like three years since I had seen him or even talked to him. When I saw him, he told me that he had gone to rehab and was doing good. But then I guess he ended up relapsing and said that he was even worse now than he used to be, because he had progressed from pills to heroin. I ended up getting high with Zach, but I told him that I don't shoot up, the only thing I do is smoke. I didn't really care what I got high on back then; as long as it was an opiate of some kind and took away my feeling of being dope-sick, I would do it. If there was one person from our friend group that knew the struggle and pain that Zach went through with his addiction first-hand it was me, unfortunately.

Our friendship was like a carousel. One of us would be up doing pretty good and the other would be down, and then we would like switch places, until the end of his life, when we were both doing bad. Looking back on it, most of our memories involved us getting intoxicated in one way or the other. I wish that wasn't reality, but we both started at a young age, and it only progressed from there.

About ten days after I saw Zach, he hit me up and told me that he was going to go to rehab again. I was really happy for him, even though I wasn't ready to get clean just yet myself. He said the only problem though was that he had to wait for a bed to open up and that it was going to be about a 45-day wait. I couldn't believe that they told him to just hang in there for 45 days after he was brave enough to ask for help.

Five days after that, I found out that Zach had overdosed and died. I was absolutely freaking crushed and was in complete shock, and thought it had to be some kind of sick joke. Like I had just seen him, and he was supposed to be getting help and moving on with his life. And now, he'd lost his life. The worst part about it was the fact that I was still getting high on the thing that had just killed my best friend. Like, what was wrong with me? How could I still do it after it just took his life? The answer: That's what addiction is. It's like a nebulous, which means it's hard to define. Nothing about addiction makes sense. The decisions we make in active addiction are non-sensible. A rational thinking person would not do almost any of the crazy things that an addicted mind would do.

I went to Zach's funeral and I couldn't help but feel guilt and shame. I couldn't even stand up and share a memory of us because I was so worried that someone would be able to tell that I was high and would kick me out.

After a really rough next few years of addiction and Covid

and homelessness, I finally got clean and got into recovery. For the longest time, I used to worry about trying to get clean, because in the back of my mind I was thinking if I try to stop like Zach did and they didn't have a bed ready for me too, was I also going to die? I really do try so hard to be an optimistic person and find at least one good thing out of every situation, even if the circumstances are tragic.

I reflected on Zach's death for years and tried so hard just to find even the smallest positive that could come from it. But I couldn't, it was impossible. There was nothing positive at all to come from it.

Until about two years ago, when I made a post about Zach on social media. I was talking about how he was brave enough to admit that he had a problem and that how we as a society had failed him. His mom Jennifer saw the post and reached out to me, and we have become close and bonded over Zach ever since. So there it was, the impossible was no more. She was the positive part that I was searching for from a tragic situation. Just like how I want to help other people by sharing my story, she wants to do the same, but for parents who have had to endure that unimaginable heartbreak of losing a child and the years of grief that follow. I'm so appreciative of her and the many conversations that we have had.

Zach, your mom is an amazing kind-hearted woman. She was lucky to have you as a son. But you were also lucky to have her as a mom. I am truly humbled and forever grateful that Jennifer has agreed to write a letter to Zach and let me include it in this book. If it weren't for her and all of her help with the pictures and letters, this tribute would not have been possible. Thank you so much for helping me complete this!

Some people, when they think about me or Zach, may think that we are just an addict and that's all we are. Did we struggle with addiction? Yes, we did! But just because we struggled with something, that doesn't define who we are as a person. He was so much more than "just an addict." He was a son, a big brother, grandchild, cousin, nephew, friend, companion, confidant, he was the one who made you laugh when you were sad. He was the one that would go out of his way to make sure everyone around him was comfortable. If you were his friend, he had your back to the fullest no matter what! He was the person that many people would turn to as their safe space. He was a light for this dark world, like a window in a dark room. But sadly, the darkness inside of him put his bright light out.

Zach had gone to rehab a couple years before his final relapse. While he was there, he wrote a letter to his addiction that is so powerful, but also so sad. I talked it over with Zach's mom and we both agreed that what more of a special way to end this tribute than with the letter that Zach wrote to the thing that ended up taking his life.

This next part will be the letter from Zach's mom, followed by the letter that Zach wrote to his addiction in his own words. Zach, since I never got up and shared a memory of us at your funeral. Please accept this as my way of honoring you. Your story still has the potential to help people and change lives even from beyond the grave. Together, we will bring awareness. My brotha, until we meet again… love you my dude! We all miss you! I promise you that I will share all of the big moments of my life with your mom just like you would have!

Jennifer's Letter

When Kory told me that he was writing a book, and asked me if he could dedicate it to my son Zach, I was honored. If this book will help others, I am all in. Kory wanted me to write a letter to Zach or write about him. I am doing both, I wanted the readers to know about him and what an amazing person and beautiful soul he had.

When I was 22, I found out that I was two months pregnant. I didn't know because I used to work out a lot and didn't get periods. I went to the clinic, and the nurse came in to let me know. First thing she said was, "Do you want an abortion?" I kind of freaked out because I had just found out. I wanted to think about it and talk to my boyfriend. I called him right away and he said the same thing the nurse did. I was deflated. I did not know if I was ready for a baby, but I also wasn't ready to end my pregnancy. I talked to my parents and we kept the baby. This was the best decision I ever made.

One night I went to meet up with my boyfriend, I walked in the room and saw him with others and a pile of cocaine. I freaked out and told him it was that, or me and this baby. Well, it is sad to say but he did not pick us. I went to live with my parents and made sure I did everything to keep my child healthy and safe. Zach was born two weeks late and he was worth the wait. He was the cutest of course. Being a new mom is hard and even more challenging because he never slept. I had to bounce him to rock music to fall asleep for 15-30 minutes at a time, then he was up for hours. As he got older, he got better and slept all the time. I tried to be the best mom for him I could be and maybe I tried to compensate for his dad not being around. I thought maybe that contributed to the problems, when he started getting in trouble.

The first time he was drunk he was 13 years old. The guy from our activity center called me to let me know he was wandering the streets and was almost hit by a car. He was grounded for a while, and once he was free, he got in trouble [again]. He was huffing the tar you put in the tires when you changed them, stealing his girlfriend's mom's pills, sneaking out of the house and going to parties. And of course when the cops came, he was the only one getting arrested.

He graduated from high school and got into college, which was exciting and scary all at the same time. He had been doing better and was excelling in school. I remember the day, it was Thanksgiving, and my good friend called me and said her nephew knew Zach from college. Then she proceeded to let me know that he was doing Oxy and partying a lot. After the call I was so upset and didn't eat and noticed that he did not either. I talked to him, and he of course denied it and said he was fine and not doing that much. Whatever that meant.

A few months later he called me and said he needed help, that he was out of control and was not sleeping or eating. His drug addiction was taking over. As a parent you never want to hear this. I left work, packed my suitcase, and went to pick him up at school. It was about a five-hour drive and of course adrenaline was driving me. On the way down I heard a song by Rascal Flats, "I Won't Let Go." I played that song repeatedly and cried the whole way. My son is everything and I wanted to be there as much as I could for him and just grab him in my arms and make him OK. When I got there, we went to a doctor that tried to help but we ended up coming back home and started looking for a rehab center.

I was on the phone for three days straight calling every place I could find. In state and out of state. We finally got a call back that a bed was open and that we had to be there by 9 a.m. the next day or it would be gone. We packed up and left at 5 p.m. for an eight-hour drive. The next morning, I admitted Zach to the rehab center and then had to drive home, leaving a piece of my heart and hoping for the best.

We couldn't talk to him while he was going through detoxing. This not knowing how he was doing was so hard and was the longest week of my life. On day 10 he called and said they wanted us to go for Parents' Day. My parents, daughter, and I packed up and were on our way. I was excited and apprehensive at the same time, not knowing what to expect. Was he the same as I left him or was he back to the son that I knew? When he approached us, he was Zach again. I was so happy and cried all at the same time. We went to some counseling meeting with him and a group session with all the attendees. He of course had made new friends and seemed so good. This is where he wrote the letter to his drug. He also wrote to his grandpa, his biological dad, and a friend that died that he was close to.

After 30 days it was time to take him home. For one I would like to say that it is not even enough time for anyone to break a habit like this. I am not sure why the government or insurance thinks that is enough time and is all they will pay for. I believe all rehabs should be at least one year minimum.

Zach was home for a few months then my cousin got him a great job in Vail at The Sabastion, a ski resort where he worked in the hospitality department. He was amazing at this job and did extremely well and advanced quickly. After being there for a few months, one of his friends joined him working there. I am not sure if that was the best thing for Zach. They started drinking and partying and eventually Zach got a DWI.

So here we go again, bailing him out, paying for lawyers, court costs, interlock expenses, traveling back and forth. Zach ended up changing jobs and going to Denver where he met his girlfriend. Things were going good and Zach signed up for art school. He loved it and was doing well till he found out that his girlfriend was pregnant, and instead of talking to him, she took it upon herself to get an abortion. This devastated him and later he told me that he thought of me and that could have been him. He wanted to be a dad so bad and would have been the best dad. His girlfriend was smoking crack and the thought of what she did drove him back to that feeling of numbing the pain.

Once he was back at it, it was almost every day. That OMG as all parents of an addict know—all the stories and lies that they are told to make you feel guilty, sorry for them, or pressured to give them money. Trust me, I have heard them all. At this point I was never really sleeping and every time the phone rang, I thought it was the call that he was gone. One night I had this strange feeling of calling him. I called all night long till 4 a.m. He finally called me and said, "Mom I need help." He was in an alley half-clothed and out of it. I told him that it was time for him to come home and I would come and get him.

There, we packed up all his and his girlfriend's stuff and brought both Zach and her to my house. Her parents picked her up a couple days later and of course blamed Zach for her drug abuse. We called everywhere again to get him into a rehab, and it took weeks, which felt like eternity. He went to a program and was doing great. He always knew how to impress the counselors and nurses. While he was there, he had to apply for jobs for when he got out. He got a great job lined up at the local golf course and his grandpa couldn't be more excited for him.

Zach was his grandpa's everything. He probably loved him more than me. Zach and my dad were extremely close and they both loved playing golf. My dad had Zach on the golf course at five, where Zach would find lost balls and sell them to the golfers for money. Zach has always been a comedian and a good salesman. Full of life and laughter.

When the season ended, he ended up getting a job at a restaurant in a local community 20 minutes from our home. He was doing great for a few weeks. Then I noticed a change. He was spending more time in his room and falling asleep a lot. He said it was because he was so tired from the new job, which I believed. One day our house was broken into while I was at work. They only stole DVD movies, some money I had in my jewelry box, and a Coach purse I had. It was so weird, why not the TVs or my jewelry? Later I found out—and always had my suspicions—that it was Zach that staged the robbery.

In October, I got home from work early and went into Zach's room to see how he was. He was laying on his bed out of it with a needle hanging out of his arm. I freaked out and woke him up. Thankfully he did wake up, but I was so devastated and taken aback that he was back to doing drugs. I was so mad and sad. I told him this was not happening in my home. Every ounce of my being wanted to kick him out, but he is also my son, my first born, the first human to love me unconditionally and that I love with all my heart unconditionally. What if he was shooting up on the street and overdosed? I would never know. I would be devastated. He is my son—good, bad, or indifferent. Addiction is a disease and as much as I tried to keep it from him, it was a part of him. If he had an eating disorder or gambling addiction, I would have felt the same and tried to help him as much as possible.

Once he was able to talk, we had a good conversation about him relapsing and why. He told me that he was depressed, he had no friends or a girlfriend, that he was not a good person, and that God did not love him and he just wanted to die. That broke my heart and I told him that I would be lost without him and that he was a good person that deserved better and to stay strong and let's get help. He was over 26 years old and had no insurance so this task was next to impossible. We tried all over for weeks. We heard of a detox place he could go to and at least be under supervision. That took weeks to get in. Once he was finally in, he was in a room with a convicted felon that was threatening to kill him in his sleep. For one, it is hard enough detoxing from drugs, in this case heroin was what Zach was doing, but to be scared for your life [too]. He ended up calling me to come and get him because he did not feel safe. So, I did. The search continued.

I asked Zach, since we can't find a place, if he could detox on his own and I would help him. He said he could try but it would be hard. That night was the longest night ever. I have never seen him in so much pain. I sat beside him as he tossed and turned all night, his legs twitching and jolting, his back hurting; he was screaming and crying. I was trying to stay strong for him, but I was dying inside. I had to leave the room for a while and break down. After hours of this unmanageable pain, he gave up and said, "Mom I can't do it." I told him it was OK and we can try something else. *At least he tried*, I said to myself as he left to go get his fix.

A few days later I was getting ready for work and saw a story on the local news about a place that was helping people in an outpatient program. I don't know if it was a sign or what, but I wrote down the number and we called. They got him in the next week. We went to the appointment together and they talked to us about the program. He would have to detox at home, but this time he had pills to help get through the pain and nausea. This time it was going better than last time. I remember he was sitting on the couch with us watching a movie and just started vomiting on himself and the couch. All I remember is him saying "I'm sorry, mom." I told him it was OK and I just wanted him to get better, it is just a couch and we can clean it.

Even writing this now makes me cry eight years after it happened. He was so thoughtful and loving and I could see the real him coming back. He made it through the detox this time and was able to start eating, and he slept for the first time in a long time. We got him to shower, which he hated. He said that the water hurt when it hit his skin. We went to his appointment, and his counseling session. He was doing great and had a positive attitude. Yes, on an outpatient program. He started the program on May 30th and did great till he started getting bored. He was not working at this time, but we were trying to keep him busy helping his grandpa in the yard. I felt that I finally had my son back. He was engaging with us and having dinner with us, playing family game night, helping around the house, and playing with his puppy he loved so much.

Then June 29th happened, I remember everything about that day. I had to go do some stuff for work then was going to meet Zach and my daughter for lunch at a local restaurant that we went to a lot. That lunch will always mean the most to me. I had a weird feeling about Zach, and that he was a little different. He was going to go to my dad's to mow the lawn and I had to get back to work.

My mom called me and said that Zach was asking for money. I called him to see what he needed money for, and he said that he wanted to go to the movies. I said not to give him the money and that I would go with him. He got mad and said never mind. He went home and he and my husband were talking on the back patio. My husband had just driven in from Salt Lake City and said he was going to take a nap. Zach said, "Me too."

I called Zach around 3:30 p.m. and he was fine at that time. I left work at 5 p.m. and my daughter called me asking where I was. I told her I was driving home and she said that I needed to hurry because it was Zach, he was dead. My whole world stopped and I don't even know how I got home. When I pulled up, the fire department and police were there. All I wanted to do was go inside but they wouldn't let me.

My daughter said that she got home and knocked on Zach's door to see what he wanted for dinner and heard his dog Hagen crying. She opened the door and saw him lying there with a needle in his arm. She immediately got the Narcan. Nothing. She gave him a second dose and nothing. She called 911 and she continued to do CPR on him till they arrived. He was gone.

My worst nightmare had happened. When they finally let me in to see him, he was laying there in a body bag. I fell to my knees and just held him and told him I loved him and now he won't have to hurt anymore. That image of him will be forever in my mind. For my dad it is him doing the yard work, looking sad and depressed. I am not sure if other parents feel this way but after he passed, I didn't know what to do with myself. I was so used to worrying about him and calling him all day long. I felt lost. It was like I was addicted to him. With the high and anxiety of not getting a hold of him, and when I did, the feeling of relief. I turned all my focus to my daughter to fill that void till she had to tell me, "Mom, I am not Zach and I am OK." I broke down.

I believe that maybe he could have received the help he needed the first time he went to rehab but not this 30- and 45-day program crap, an addict needs to go for a year minimum. That way they learn a new way of life. But those programs are $30k, who has that kind of money just laying around? Not this paycheck-to-paycheck family. Looking back, I wish I could have sent him there, maybe he would still be here, and I wouldn't have to write about him in a book. The drug epidemic in the USA is real, and I wish the government would see that and do more to help.

I miss my son every day! He was an incredible person with a big heart and could have been very successful if he didn't have that demon inside him. He sends me signs all the time in songs, feathers on the ground when I think of him, bringing Kory into my life and in my dreams. The first dream I had about Zach was that he came to me and was all in white with huge white wings. His back was to me because he was getting his wings. He turned around and looked at me and said, "Don't worry about me, mom, I will be OK," and I woke up.

Dear Zach, I want to tell you that you are the best son a mom could have, and I would never go back and change the decision I made to have you. I loved you from the moment I found out that I was going to be a mom. I miss you every day, but I know that I will see you again and you are always in my heart.

Love, Mom

To My Addiction

First off, I want to say I hate you for how much destruction you and I have caused together. I hate that I did not choose you. You dwelled deep inside of me and I was blind to see it. I hate that all I had to do to give you power over me was to give you one drink, one puff, just one taste to instantly make me fall in love. I hate the lengths and hoops I jumped through to keep you in control over me, and I just sat back and let you. But I'm taking my power back from you. I am no longer giving you what you need. I am no longer going to lie, cheat, and steal for you. I am no longer going to go broke for you. I am no longer going to break the law to have you in my life. You have tried to kill me before and failed. If I continue to live my life for you, I will surely die. In the past I may have not cared if this happened, but I have learned to love myself more than I love you. I was once your biggest ally. I hope you are ready for me to be your greatest enemy, because I am now stronger than you.

Remember the date 8-27-12, because that is the last day that you are going to have the benefit of getting what you want. We will no longer hurt those that love us the most. I will no longer destroy my body for you. You will no longer get the fuel you need to burn inside of me. I want to tell you that I hate you with a much stronger passion than I loved you. You made me feel like I was not a good person, and I now know that you feed off my weakness. Well, I am no longer weak, I no longer hate myself, and I'm going to use every ounce of that hate against you. I hope you've enjoyed our time together because those times are over. I've found the tools to have a much better life than you could ever offer and you best believe that I intend to use them. So one last time, goodbye old friend. I hate you with every fiber of my being and it's time for you to die. So remember that date, because it's the last time we will be seeing each other.

—Zach Montoya

In Loving Memory
Jonathan <u>Zachary</u> Montoya
5/9/1990 - 6/29/2018

Photos

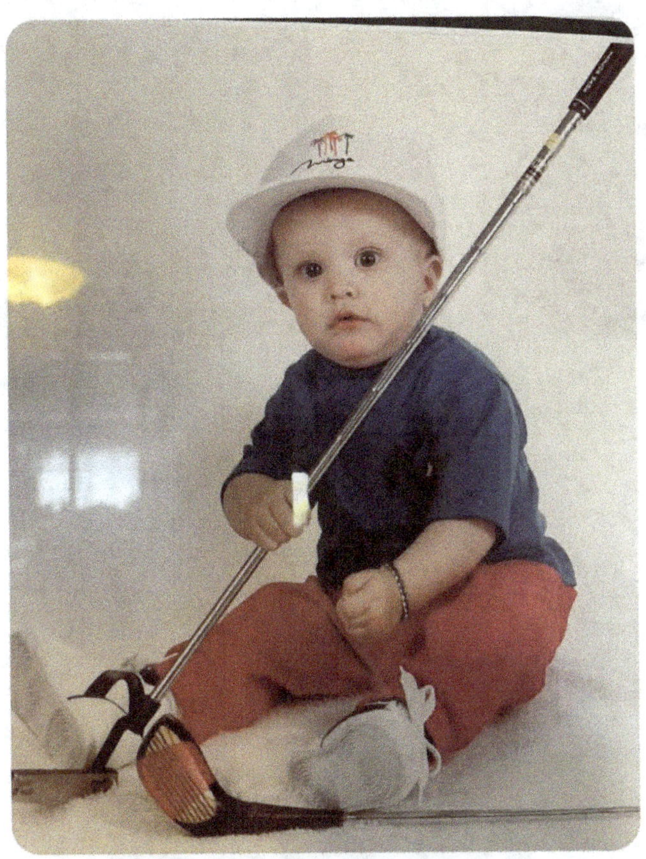

This is Zach's one-year-old picture, of course with a golf club. We tried to recreate this for his senior picture.

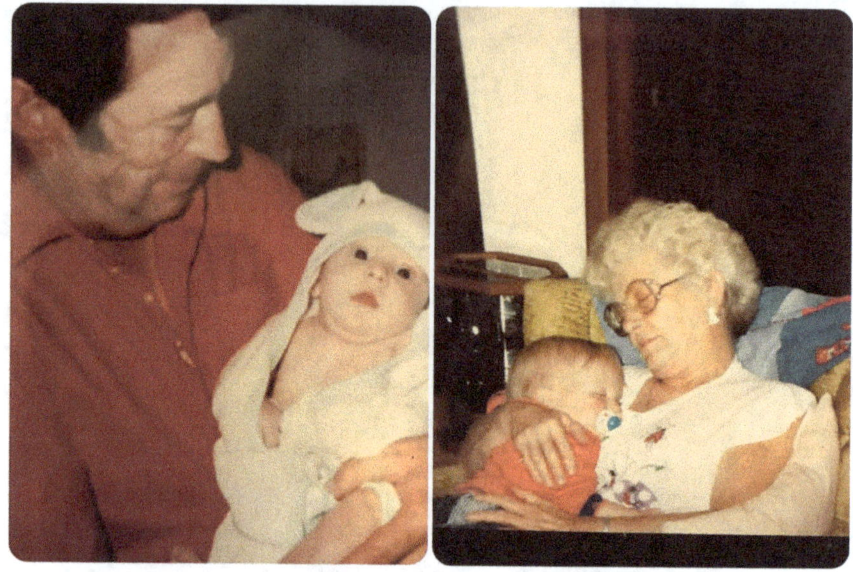

Left: Zach's grandpa giving Zach a bath. Right: Zach sleeping on his GG. She would care for him during the day.

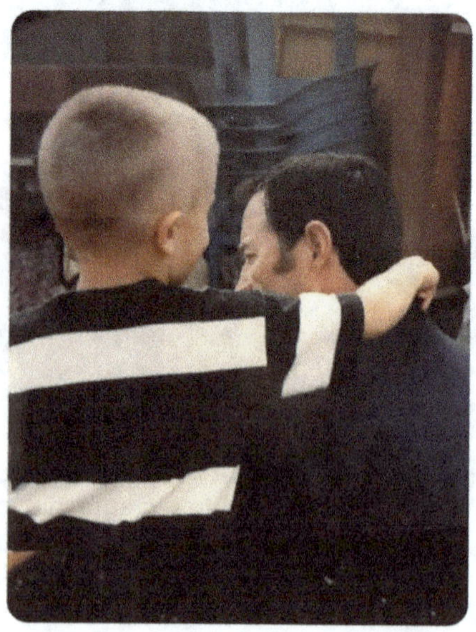

Zach and his grandpa at the zoo. I just see the bond they had.

His goofy grin. 2 years old.

This was at a ride at the state fair. I think he was 3.

This is when I married Taylor's dad. All he wanted to do is squirt the trees outside 'cause he did on the wedding the day before.

Zach holding his baby sister.

Easter Day, Zach helping Taylor ride her tricycle.

Zach just looks so happy. He just lost his tooth. He was
probably 6.

Family photo. Zach was 9 and Taylor was 4.

Zach and Taylor.

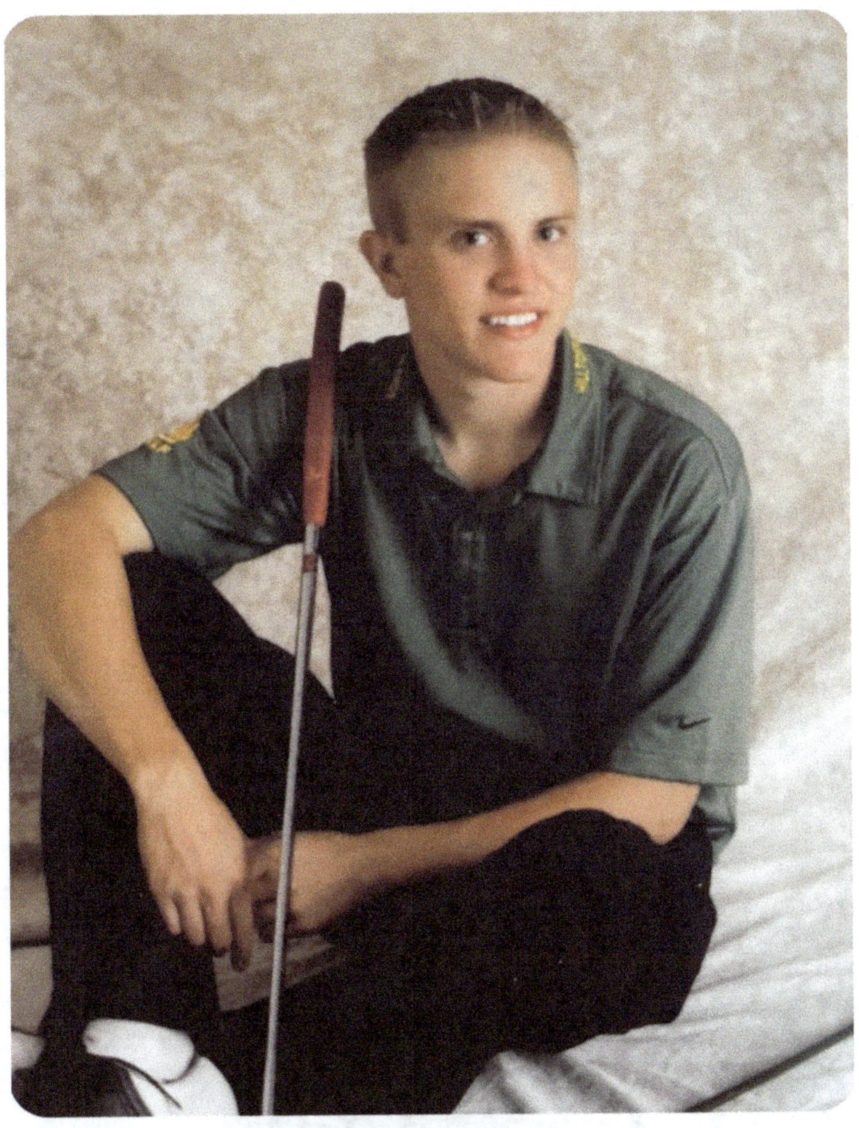

Zach's senior picture. Photo reenactment 17 years later.

Graduation 2008, Blaise, Zach, and Sean. Friends since first grade.

Zach and his high-school sweetheart, Jen

2008, when we dropped off Zach at NMSU. I cried the whole
way home.

This was the best picture. Zach heading out after my wedding
to Lee. 10/24/2011.

This is from college, probably at some concert .

Good times, good friends! In photo from left to right: Kristina, Zach, Kev Q, Andrew, Kate

I love this one. Zach was working at the Howl at the Moon Bar
and Grill in Denver. He was doing great until he called to tell
me tables would dine and ditch, and he needed money.

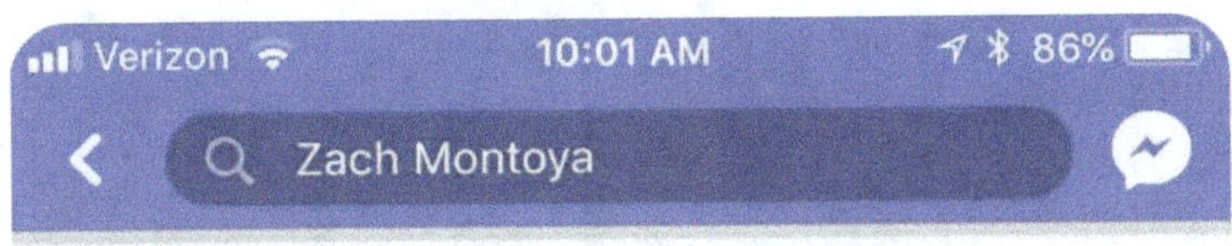

Happy birthday to the best mom I could ask for!

The freshest coors you can drink. Cheers mama

Taylor and I went to visit him in Arvada, CO. We went to
Golden to the Coors tasting. He posted this and it came up
after he posted it again. Cried my eyes out.

Last picture I have of Zach's grandma and Zach. She had this
on her phone and I found it after she passed.

This was a year after he passed, his mom sending her love.

Taylor sending a lantern balloon to her brother Zach.

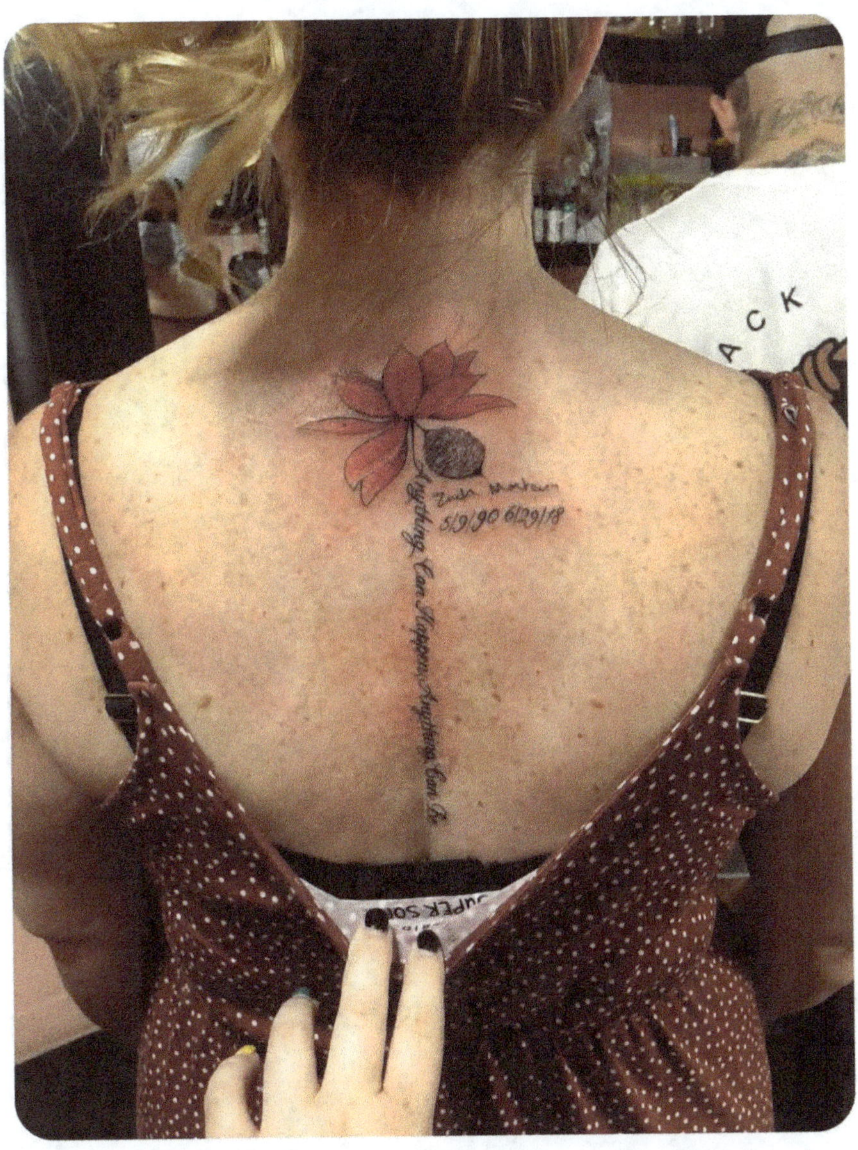

Jennifer's tattoo for Zach. "I was trying to think of something, and I got a sympathy card with a lotus flower, so that was the flower. It has his thumbprint, his name in his writing, and his dates of birth and death. The wording is from his tattoo on his arm. It is from a Shel Silverstein poem, 'Anything can happen; anything can be.'"

Global Dance Festival 2010 at Red Rocks Amphitheatre. Matt, Kory, Zach, Martin.

Kory and Zach's mom Jennifer in Phoenix after eating dinner
and discussing the book.

This is one of my favorite photos of Zach! I feel like this picture
embodies perfectly the spirit and joy for life that he had. He
truly was the life of the party, both literally and metaphorically,
and he will be forever missed! In the photo are Zach, Kory, and
Matt. All three of us were really good friends! "EDC Vegas"
2011 night 3, One of the best nights ever!

Acknowledgments

A huge thank you to Leya Booth for your professionalism and enthusiasm that you had for my book. She helped me from start to finish, with the editing and book layout and went above and beyond to make sure that everything was done exactly how I wanted it!

And a special shoutout to Vaughn Hale for creating the custom graphic design image for the cover that helped make my vision come to life.

ABOUT THE AUTHOR

Kory Wade Nelson is an author from Albuquerque, NM. He was born in Idaho Falls, ID. He currently resides in Phoenix, AZ. His desire to help people is seen clearly through his writing, as he hopes to motivate others by emboldening them on their own journey toward healing and personal growth. Helping people find the strength and self-belief that they can overcome their addiction is his purpose in life. By sharing his story, he hopes to encourage people who feel lost, broken, or alone. His passion is reminding others that recovery and transformation and eventually evolution, are possible. His mission is simple: Save one life at a time! He writes to inspire hope, healing, and second chances. He believes real, genuine, personal stories are important because people can relate to them and it makes people feel understood and gives them the strength to keep going. One day at a time. He is currently 3 years, and 9 months clean off Fentanyl.